How to Help Your Child Do a Science Fair Project: A Beginner's Guide for Parents or Guardians of Children in the Elementary through Middle Grades

William J. Sumrall

Illustrations by Tom Grosskopf
Lafayette High School Art Teacher

Foreword

The most important question you should ask before purchasing this book is, "How does it differ from the many science fair books on the market?"

Most books that claim to be about science fairs do not prepare children to do a project. Many offer the reader a book full of science activities instead of a step-by-step guide to science fair success. While these books may be great resources for finding a project idea, they fail to relate the nuts and bolts of developing a successful science fair project.

The author of this book, Dr. William J. Sumrall, professor of science education at the University of Mississippi, has been involved in science fairs in multiple capacities for more than 30 years. His experience and roles include:
- Eight years of service as a state science and engineering fair director
- Thirty years of judging science and engineering fairs at every level:
    - International judging
    - Best of Fair judging at regional and state levels
    - Category judging at regional and state levels
    - Yearly K-12 judging at schools in Florida, Illinois, Louisiana, and Mississippi
- Regional Scientific Review Committee member
- Multiple publications on the topic of science fairs
- High school science fair coordinator
- Multiple workshops and presentations about science fairs

Contents

1: Is My Data Quantifiable?

2: What Kind of Graph Do I Use and How Do I Display It?

3: Where Do I Get My Idea?

4: Does My Project Have a Purpose?

5: What Controls and Other Variables Should I Consider?

6: What Makes My Project Better than Another?

7: Is My Project Safe and Does It Follow the Rules?

8: How Do I Put It All Together?

Epilogue: Why Do a Science Fair Project?

1: Is My Data Quantifiable?

Does your child have a science fair project idea? Whether they came up with the idea on their own or got it from a book, the Internet, a teacher, a friend, a sibling, a person off the street, or you, the first question that should be asked is whether the project will yield numeric data that can be graphed. Before getting started with an idea, consider the following:

- Can I measure changes in length?
- Can I measure changes in volume?
- Can I measure changes in mass or weight?
- Can I measure rate (e.g., a change over time)?
- Can I measure temperature?
- Can I count something?

While you don't have to do all of these things in your project, you probably need to do at least one of them to be able to graph data.

Scientists tend to be objective thinkers. While they may have opinions and consider possibilities, they, for the most part, like to look at numbers. An example of a common science fair project I have judged that tends to be subjective—not objective—is "Which laundry detergent works best?"

In this experiment, children will stain white strips of cloth with mustard, coffee, dirt, and anything else they can find to determine which detergent will clean best. While the idea meets a lot of criteria for being a really good project, as I will explain later, it tends to come up short with regard to answering the most important question: which laundry detergent really DOES work best?

Students tend to "eyeball" the cloth strips after washing and give an opinion as to which detergent cleaned the best. Scientists do not work that way. As a parent, you need to guide your child to either figure out a way to get numeric data from their experiment or go with another project idea.

Can "Which laundry detergent works best?" be quantified? Sure it can. But this may require buying something called a turbidity meter, which measures water's cloudiness, to make that determination. If one measures what gets left behind after stirring dirty strips of cloth in a mixture of detergent and water, it's possible to get a numeric value of liquid cloudiness. However, in addition to the expense of buying a turbidity meter, this particular project is wrought with control issues—an important topic that I will discuss in Chapter 5.

Other experiments that tend not to be quantified very well include:

- Which type of bread molds fastest?
- What temperature causes bread to mold fastest?
- What is the relationship between apple browning and temperature?
- Which nail polish lasts the longest?
- Which liquid stains teeth the most?
- Which soft drink has the most fizz?
- Which potato chip brand has the most grease?
- Which battery lasts the longest?
- Does salt water freeze slower than fresh water?

There are likely one or more ways to get quantifiable data for each of these questions. If you can figure out a way to measure these questions such that data can be graphed, then they certainly can be made into good elementary science fair projects. But difficulty to control for variables, and, in some cases, the time it takes to collect the data (have you ever sat around waiting for a flashlight's batteries to cease working?) make the results of these projects difficult to measure and quantify.

Scientists do use what is called qualitative data from time to time. Qualitative data is usually observational data that may or not be able to be graphed. Open-ended survey data and general observations regarding the senses of smell, taste, feel, etc. are examples of possible qualitative data. It is OK for a science fair project to include some general observational data, but the best projects have more precise data that can be put into graph format.

2: What Kind of Graph Do I Use and How Do I Display It?

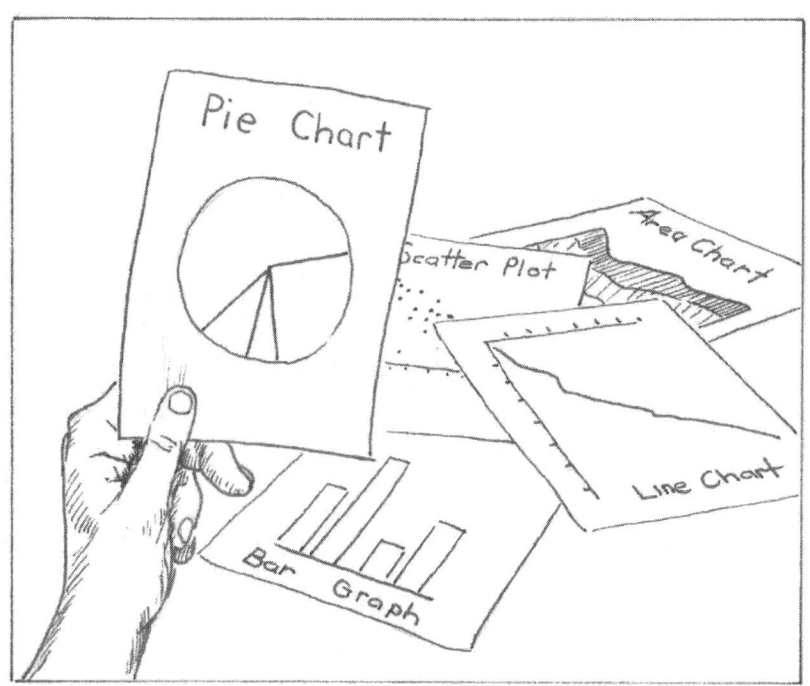

OK, your child has an idea that allows for quantifiable testing and measurement. Thus, numeric data are abundant and ready for graphing. But a big decision point involves the type of graph needed. And, perhaps more importantly, how the data get displayed with regard to variables, trials, and the intervals along an x/y axis.

The following are some common mistakes when it comes to graphing.

Mistake #1: A line graph is used when a bar/column graph would show the results better.

The purpose of creating a graph is to show trends and relationships in the data. Understanding the changes or lack of changes helps explain the results and helps one make predictions.

Generally, line graphs are used to display changes over time, while bar graphs are used to display and compare frequency counts. Pie graphs are used to display frequencies in a fractional/percentage format.

Examples of data suited for a line graph include:

- Temperature changes over time
- Speed and velocity changes
- Changing swing rates of a pendulum
- Plant growth measurements over time
- Timed movements of an insect or other invertebrate animal through a maze

Examples of data suited for a bar graph include:

- Final plant growth measurements after manipulating a variable (e.g., fertilizer, light, temperature, etc.)

- Food preferences of insects or other invertebrate animals (e.g., honey, sugar, etc.)
- Paper towel strength/absorbency
- Popcorn kernel popping comparisons
- Strength of glue

Mistake #2: The x/y axis and/or fractions within a pie graph are not labeled.

Graphs are used to pictorially explain your results. Without labeled axes, it is difficult for a teacher or judge to understand what the lines or bars on the graph mean. Similarly, displaying a pie graph without labels makes it impossible for the viewer to know what the fraction pieces represent.

Mistake #3: The axis is labeled incorrectly.

Three reasons to display data in a graph are to show changes over time, frequency, and fractions/percentages. In the case of both line and bar graphs, the variable that is physically manipulated by the experimenter (known as the independent or manipulated variable) gets placed along the x-axis. And the variable that the experimenter measures (known as the dependent or responding variable) gets placed along the y-axis. Thus, in a line graph, the viewer is able to see changes over time from left to right. In a bar graph, the viewer is able to see changes vertically, allowing for increase/decrease comparisons.

Mistake #4: The intervals are too small or large to best show the data.

When developing a graph to display data, one must set the right intervals on the x-y axis. Generally, these intervals are determined <u>after</u> data have been collected.

Setting the intervals involves helping your child decide on a reasonable range that shows the data. This requires thinking about the minimum and maximum numbers to be placed along an axis such that the data are not displayed too "scrunched" nor too "stretched."

For example, one activity in which I collect data to be graphed in line form involves testing the relationship between beaker size and a candle staying lit. The beakers I use to cover a lit candle are 50 ml, 100 ml, 250 ml, 600 ml, and 1,000 ml. The time the candle stays lit once covered varies from 2 to 38 seconds. As shown in Figure 1, I used intervals of 100 ml for the independent/manipulated variable and 10 seconds for the dependent/responding variable.

Figure 1. Line Graph: Relationship Between Beaker Size and Candle Staying Lit

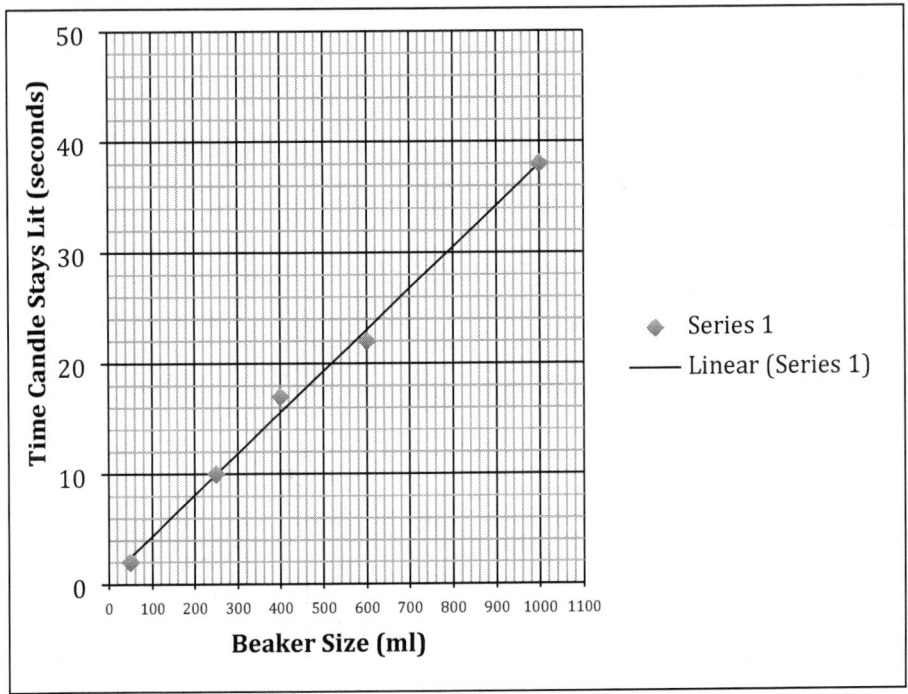

Similarly, if creating a bar graph to compare the number of popcorn kernels that go un-popped by brand, you need to help your child form the graph after the data have been collected. The y-axis on the graph in Figure 2 uses intervals of 5 based on the fact that the number of un-popped kernels ranged between 5 and 48. This range is the result of testing three types of microwave popcorn brands using three trials per brand.

Figure 2. Bar Graph: Comparison of Un-popped Popcorn Kernels by Brand

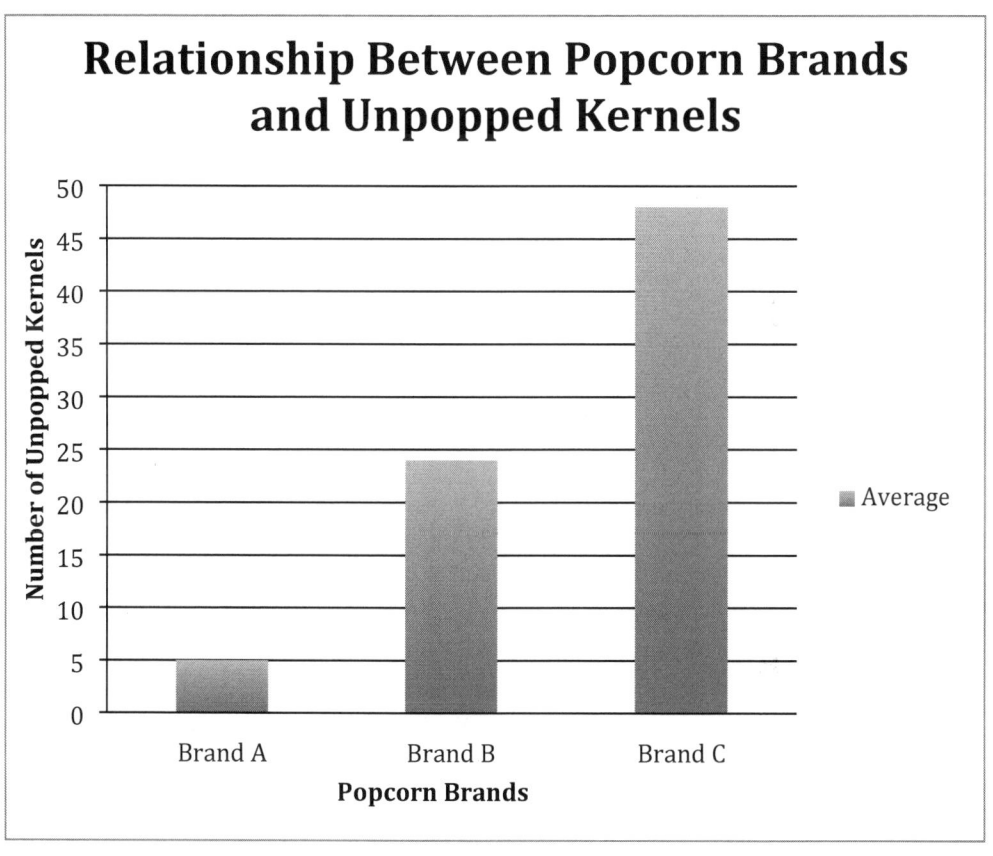

Mistake #5: The trials are not averaged.

When judging projects, I have seen students plot multiple trials on their graphs. However, it is much easier to understand and interpret trial data in a line or bar graph if the averaged data from the trials get plotted instead.

The data displayed in Figure 2 are averages. Table 1 displays the data used to derive these averages.

Table 1. Un-popped Kernel Data From 3 Trials of 3 Brands

Brand	Trial 1 # Un-popped Kernels	Trial 2 # Un-popped Kernels	Trial 3 # Un-popped Kernels	Average
Brand A Popcorn	7	5	3	5
Brand B Popcorn	28	25	19	24
Brand C Popcorn	50	52	42	48

As another example: the data in Table 2 result from changing a pendulum's string length to see how this changed the rate of swings per minute. In the interest of time, the number of swings was measured in 15-second trials. The final number of swings per minute was calculated by multiplying the average times 4.

Table 2. Rate Changes Due to Changing String Length

String Length	Trial 1 # Swings/15 sec	Trial 2 # Swings/15 sec	Trial 3 # Swings/15 sec	Average # Swings/15 sec	Swings/ Min
20 cm	14	14	14	14	56
40 cm	11	11	11	11	44
60 cm	9	9	9	9	36

A line graph showing the relationship between string length and pendulum rate is displayed in Figure 3. Notice the intervals selected, where the independent and dependent variables are placed on the axis, and how only the trial averages are used to show how the rate changes.

Figure 3. Line Graph: Relationship Between String Length and Pendulum Rate

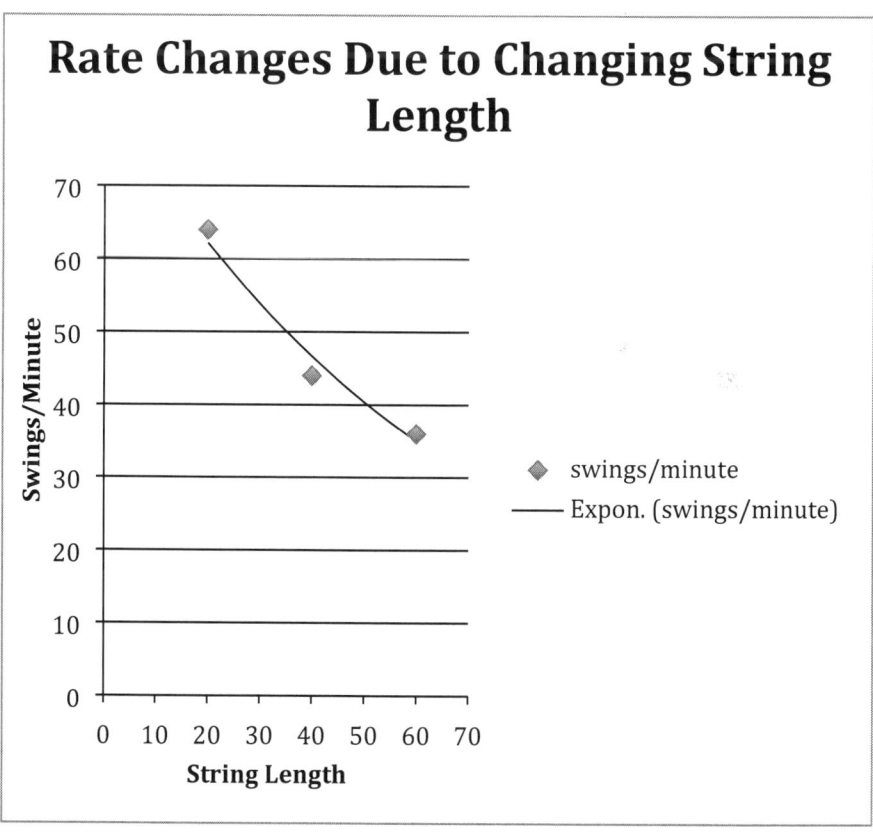

Mistake #6: The reasons for outlying data caused by possible experimental error are not considered.

A sign of a good experiment is when data are consistently repeated among trials. This tells the scientist that whatever factor has been manipulated is causing the change. In the pendulum experiment, the fact that all three trials yielded the same results when the string length was increased (as shown in Table 2) is a good thing. Based on that, a "scientist" (i.e., student) can definitively say that increasing string length slows down the pendulum and results in fewer swings in a minute's time.

However, if the data go "all over the place," as shown in Table 3, the student needs to try to determine why the tests were not consistent. In addition to doing more trials, the student may need to consider experimental error as a possible reason for the lack of consistency in the data. Perhaps there was slippage of the string between trials and the student didn't measure the string length each time. Maybe the pendulum hit something as it swung. There are a number of possible reasons why the data might not be consistent. Additional reflection may be required in terms of controlling for every possible factor. For example, did the student think to control for the angle at which they dropped the pendulum?

Table 3. Rate Changes Due to Changing String Length

String Length	Trial 1 # Swings/15 sec	Trial 2 # Swings/15 sec	Trial 3 # Swings/15 sec	Avgerage # Swings/15 sec	Swings/min
20 cm	14	14	20		
40 cm	13	11	15		
60 cm	9	13	18		

3: Where Do I Get My Idea?

Possibly the most stressful part of doing a science fair project for the child, the parent or guardian, and, believe it or not, the teacher, is developing an idea. As a former middle school teacher, it was a real challenge to help a classroom of students develop a project idea that met all the rules and regulations. While children are often told "Your project should be based on something you're interested in doing," there are caveats that come with this piece of advice.

Telling a child to do their project on something that interests them is OK only to a certain extent. Science fair rules and regulations are rightfully such that all project ideas need to be safe for both the child and others who may be involved in the project (safety will be discussed in the next chapter).

In most cases, an elementary-level project should not involve vertebrate (including human) animals. So, if your child wants to do a project on their pet dog (e.g., "Does my dog prefer table scraps over dog food?"), I would advise you to encourage them to choose another idea. While there is paperwork to permit such experimentation, my opinion is that it is not worth the difficulty of trying to gain approval to do a project of this type. I advise avoiding both humans and animals with backbones when coming up with a project idea. Surveying human and vertebrate animal parts (e.g., teeth, hair, etc.) is included on the list of ideas that should be nixed unless you want to go through the cumbersome process of completing a lot of paperwork to gain approval.

So how can you help your child find a project idea? In an ideal world, you would like for your child to come up with something completely original. (This is called doing science through inquiry.) However, having judged fairs for over 30 years I can say that for the science fair beginner, there are very few original ideas or questions. Most projects get started based on ideas from parents or guardians, teachers, and others.

If you as a parent want your child to be independent in coming up with an idea, the Internet is a good starting point. There have also been many books published throughout the years that are full of science activities. Figure 4 offers a list of current resources to help your child get started.

However—and this is a big however—some of the resources on the list are only intended to be starting points. Many of the resources provide science activities but not actual experiments. Therefore, an idea from the Internet or a book may not end up being an experiment that involves any kind of testing and measurement. Activities pulled from the Internet and/or science resource books that I have commonly seen at science fairs include:

- Dyeing a white carnation through osmosis using food coloring
- Baking soda/vinegar volcanoes
- Models of the solar system
- Floating an egg in salt water
- Growing crystals

The carnation osmosis, baking soda/vinegar reaction, egg floating, and crystal growing activities can possibly be turned into test/measurement experiments, but in most cases students who present these activities at science fairs are demonstrating a science phenomenon rather than an experiment. Thus, as pointed out in Chapter 1, it is essential to keep in mind whether your project idea can be quantified such that data can be graphed.

Figure 4. Science Fair Resources List

Science Buddies
www.sciencebuddies.org

Offers a guide to the basics of doing a science fair project. Also has many different project ideas, as well as more advanced science projects.

Science Buddies: Teacher Resources
www.sciencebuddies.org/science-fair-projects/teacher_resources.shtml
Science fair resources and activities.

Science Pioneers
http://www.sciencepioneers.org/science-fair/science-fair-resources
A list of many different resources for science fair projects.

Science Fair Central
http://school.discoveryeducation.com/sciencefaircentral
Free project ideas and presentation tips.

Edutopia
www.edutopia.org/blog/science-fair-resources-parents-matt-davis
Some links to resources about science fairs.

101 Great Science Experiments: A Step-by-Step Guide
https://www.amazon.com/gp/product/1465428267/ref=pd_sim_14_9?ie=UTF8&pd_rd_i=1465428267&pd_rd_r=VGE1KM4J6FQ9FP2M4ZDV&pd_rd_w=FhNvi&pd_rd_wg=ZRroB&psc=1&refRID=VGE1KM4J6FQ9FP2M4ZDV

www.scholastic.com/teachers/article/40-cool-science-experiments-web
A list of fun science experiments from Scholastic.

STEAM Kids: 50+ Science/Technology/Engineering/Art/Math Hands-On Projects for Kids
https://www.amazon.com/STEAM-Kids-Technology-Engineering-Hands/dp/1537372041/ref=zg_bs_3224_4

Community Resources for Science
www.crscience.org/educators/ScienceFair
Great tools and resources for teachers who are planning a science fair or encouraging students to participate in one.

BrainPOP
https://educators.brainpop.com/lesson-plan/science-fair-lesson-plan-planning-projects-brainpop-brainpop-jr
A lesson plan that focuses on helping students better understand how to plan a science fair project.

"Science Fairs: Teaching Students to Think Like Scientists"
https://www.sciencenewsforstudents.org/article/science-fairs-teaching-students-think-scientists
An article that highlights the importance of science fairs.

Science Fair 911 – Tips for Teachers
http://www.stevespanglerscience.com/blog/2012/02/20/science-fair-911-tips-for-teachers
How to help students develop their projects.

4: Does My Project Have a Purpose?

After many years of judging science fairs at all levels, I have come to the conclusion that the better projects tend to have a purpose. An example of a couple of projects I judged long ago that did not have any purpose had the following titles:

> "Can you cook with Vaseline?"

> "Can women get prostate cancer?"

I remember standing there in front of the children, thinking to myself, "Why?" (The second project noted above, though it was many years ago, had to have received nothing but a blank stare from me.)

Seriously, I'm sure that in both cases I took the time to stop and ask a few questions for the students' sake in an effort to be a good judge. But I am certain that the projects, based on their titles alone, received minimal scores.

Some projects—while interesting and useful to the student—really do not find out anything. Examples of these include the types of projects in which the student does a science demonstration, not a science experiment:

- How do you make a volcano?
- How do you make an artificial lung?
- How do you make a model of the solar system?
- Can an egg float in salt water?

Collections are another project type that, while very useful for the student, really do not find out anything. Examples of these include:

- Leaf collections
- Insect collections

Good projects tend to be relevant and tied to the real world. Many are consumer goods-connected:

- Which diaper is the most absorbent?
- Which sponge soaks up the most liquid?
- Which popcorn pops the most kernels?
- Which glue is the strongest?

These examples of consumer-based projects, if done the right way, offer data that can be graphed.

5: What Controls and Other Variables Should I Consider?

Doing an experiment is a form of problem solving. It usually involves changing a variable to see what effect that change has on a system being observed. As discussed in Chapter 2, the variable being changed is referred to as either the independent or manipulated variable.

Here's a good example of an independent/manipulated variable in an experiment. In a project I judged several years ago, a second-grader investigated the effect of tire pressure on the distance her bicycle rolled down a hill onto a level surface. She, with her daddy's help, manipulated the air pressure by lessening it by roughly 10 psi after three trials.

The dependent/responding variable was the distance the bicycle rolled after each trial. The distance was measured by a trundle wheel the dad had obtained from work. This gave the student quantifiable data: the distance her bicycle rolled compared to specific levels of tire air pressure. This data is best displayed in a bar graph.

How a scientist controls for variables in an experiment is what I believe separates a good scientist from a bad one. In the example of the bike experiment, it seems like there would be few controls to worry about. However, there are actually several important controls to be considered.

One control is the path the bike is rolled on. If the incline or road smoothness differ along the paths taken, the distance the bicycle rolls can be affected. To help ensure trial consistency, the student and her dad used a rope laid out in a straight line as a means to consistently maintain a fairly straight path for rolling the bicycle.

Most of the other controls have to do with consistency regarding wind resistance. By doing all the trials on the same day, the student helped prevent the wind change effect that could have occurred if she did the trials on different days.

A wind resistance-related control that the student and her dad did not consider was consistency of posture: they didn't think about the need for her to lean over or be upright at the same angle during each trial such that her body's wind resistance was the same. Thus, with each trial and manipulation of tire air pressure, her posture was not consistent.

While the student consistently did not pedal during the trials, the position of the pedals did vary, which could have had a minor wind resistance-related impact on how far the bicycle rolled.

One major indicator that not all the variables in an experiment have been controlled for is when data points differ greatly across trials, particularly after doing multiple trials. Take, for example, an experiment that measures the breaking point of popsicle sticks that have been glued together for the purpose of determining the strength of the glue bond. Table 4 shows data a student gathered after doing multiple trials to investigate the strength of different glue bonds. He hung a bucket across glued-together popsicle sticks and recorded how many pennies the sticks were able to hold in the bucket before breaking.

Table 4. Glue Bond Strength Based on Brand

Glue Brand	Trial 1 # of Pennies	Trial 2 # of Pennies	Trial 3 # of Pennies	Average
Gorilla	1,252	1,299	434	
Elmer's	754	730	221	
Titebond	643	655	134	

Good experimental technique can be determined by the consistency of data results between trials. In the case of the glue experiment, the data suggest that the experimenter did not control for everything during the third trial for each glue brand. Perhaps he tested the popsicle sticks before the glue set, meaning the time to dry was not well-controlled. Another possibility is that the popsicle sticks were not glued together at the same distance—maybe the sticks in the first two trials were glued together 2 centimeter from the end of the stick while the sticks in the third trials got glued together 1 centimeters from the end.

If data are not consistent, the experimenter needs to do additional trials to try to determine which control(s) they are not considering. Getting data that go all over the place does not show good experimental technique!

6: What Makes My Project Better Than Another?

It's easy to go beyond traditionally bad science fair projects like making a volcano, putting together a leaf collection, or creating a model of the solar system. But after clearing that hurdle, what makes a project stand out? Having judged thousands of projects over the years and also witnessed what influences judges, I have identified 10 factors that separate the good projects from the bad. In no particular order of importance, they are:

1) The student used multiple trials when collecting data.
2) The student seems to enjoy their project.
3) The student is able to explain their project in detail.
4) The backboard is visually appealing.
5) The backboard is free of grammar and spelling issues.
6) The project took place across multiple years.
7) The backboard is large.
8) The student chose the right project category.
9) The student spent sufficient time on their project.
10) The project idea is unique.

Some of these factors, you may say, shouldn't have anything to do with how judges determine which projects are winners. And, in many cases I agree—particularly since the rubrics judges use don't include some of the items listed above. But nevertheless, judges are human, and I can assure you that these factors do influence judging scores. More detail is provided on each of the 10 items below.

1) The student used multiple trials when collecting data.

In addition to making sure the data can be graphed and are consistent among the trials, a good scientist needs to consider how many trials is enough. The answer depends on the project type. In the pendulum and popcorn experiments discussed in Chapter 2, three trials were used per variable. Assuming the numbers are consistent across the trials, that is probably enough. (If a project deals with seeds, I recommend doing more than three trials. Testing 10 seeds would probably be a good starting point.) But as stated earlier, if the trial results are inconsistent, more trials and rethinking the controls are encouraged. The more trials, the better, whatever the project. Consistency of results is important.

2) The student seems to enjoy their project.

It makes a big difference to judges when they approach a child who is smiling and happy to discuss their project. Enthusiasm and apparent enjoyment win over a judge even if the project has a few areas for improvement. Unfortunately, I have approached children who looked as if their dog had been put to sleep that morning—looking down at the floor, unwilling to describe what they did, and projecting a demeanor of not wanting to be there. It is important for parents or guardians to make sure that the project is something the child really wants to do.

3) The student is able to explain their project in detail.

First, I believe parental involvement is a really good thing when it comes to helping a child develop a science fair project. The key, though, is that when a judge asks questions the child should be able to explain everything they did while working on the project. Additionally, the child needs to have a working knowledge of the science concepts behind the project. For example, a child who investigated which microwave popcorn brand pops the most kernels might be asked why popcorn pops. (The simple scientific answer is that popcorn kernels have water inside them such that heat from a microwave causes water expansion, which causes the kernels to pop.) The bottom line is that the child needs to convince the judge that they did the majority of the project on their own and that they understand the science behind the project.

A major weakness I have found when judging is that many children have not been coached well enough to explain their project. Even if the knowledge is there, sometimes the communication skills are not. I suggest that parents or

31

guardians practice with their child to better prepare them to meet the judge.

4) The backboard is visually appealing.

I am a big believer in judging the quality of the information within a project first and foremost. That said, I have seen judges' scores vary based on the quality and neatness of a backboard's appearance. Colored borders, a cute title, typed information, computer-generated graphs, and headings large enough to be seen at a distance are some of the factors that make a difference to judges. I have even seen children color-coordinate their clothing with the colors used on their backboard. Do these factors take the idea of a science fair project too far? Perhaps, but as a science fair coordinator I have witnessed them influence judges' scores.

5) The backboard is free of grammar and spelling issues.

Judges tend to be well-educated people. Misspelling words or using "their" when you mean "there" are the types of mistakes that can sway a judge's feelings toward your project. It's a good idea to have a proofreader review your backboard before fair day arrives.

6) The project took place across multiple years.

This message is meant for children in the middle grades. For some reason, projects that continue from the previous year seem to have an advantage. That is why, as a parent or guardian, you want to make sure your child's project is something they are interested in doing. It goes back to the factor of whether the child enjoys and has enthusiasm for their project.

However, I wouldn't make my child do a multi-year project just for the sake of it, especially if they are bored with the project. I have seen first-year projects win many times, so in my opinion doing a multi-year project should not be a primary focus.

7) The backboard is large.

This is one thing I don't think should be a factor at all in determining a project's quality, but I have noticed through the years that in many cases projects with larger backboards do better. Perhaps a larger backboard gives the impression that more work has been done.

The Intel International Science and Engineering Fair organization, whose science fair guidelines are followed by many schools (and who annually holds the world's largest pre-college science competition), recommends specific backboard maximum dimensions:

- Depth (front to back): 30 inches or 76 centimeters
- Width (side to side): 48 inches or 122 centimeters
- Height (floor to top): 108 inches or 274 centimeters

8) The student chose the right project category.

While I believe projects should be done based on a child's interest, it's worth noting that there are some categories that generally receive fewer submissions—meaning less competition. While categories such as botany and environmental science are probably more competitive than others, a less-competitive category that sometimes gets offered at the local level is team projects. As a parent or guardian, you should consult with the fair director to find out which categories get offered at your school. Whether or not the director will tell you the least-competitive categories is a case of "It wouldn't hurt to ask."

9) The student spent sufficient time on their project.

Nothing impresses a judge more than a student who has spent time on project development and data collection. Obviously, some projects require more time than others. Projects related to botany/plant growth, for instance, require a lot of time. But in any case, when multiple days were spent on a project a judge will consider favorably the amount of work that went into it.

10) The project idea is unique.

Coming up with a unique project is a major challenge, as explained in Chapter 3. Having judged countless projects I have seen just about everything. While I can't give you your unique project idea, I can say that every now and then I do see a new project at a school fair. (The popcorn project I discussed has been done many times, as have other examples identified in this book.) My recommendation is to think along the lines of purpose and perhaps consumer knowledge as a starting point for a fresh idea.

7: Is My Project Safe and Does It Follow the Rules?

When it comes to science fair projects, safety is the number-one concern. A whole separate book could be written about science safety and science fairs. The Intel International Science and Engineering Fair guidelines have a rigorous set of rules. As a parent or guardian you should visit the organization's website (https://student.societyforscience.org/intel-isef-display-and-safety-regulations) to learn about what is and is not allowed during experimentation as well as what can be displayed at the fair. The forms your school will use to register students (typically those who place 1st to 3rd) for a regional fair will more than likely come from this website.

Some basic safety requirements for elementary/middle grade students are:

- No projects using flammable liquids
- No projects using drugs, tobacco, or alcohol
- No projects using microbial pathogens
- Projects must gain approval from the proper science personnel (e.g., science teacher, physician, veterinarian, etc.)
- Projects should have adult supervision
- Students should wear safety glasses and any other safety equipment deemed necessary by the adult supervisor(s) during the experimentation process

There are also general safety rules regarding displaying one's project on the day of the fair:

- No liquids, including water
- No sharp-cornered objects
- No glass
- No live animals or vertebrate specimens
- No operating high-voltage electric motors

Most children have a natural desire to display their work. It is OK in some cases to show part of the project "live," though I

36

recommend using photographs as much as possible. Other than the experimenter, no one else should appear in a photograph placed on the backboard.

In terms of non-safety-related display rules, you should check with your child's school for specific requirements. Some schools require only one size and type of backboard. Displaying grades or ribbons received prior to judging is not allowed at most school fairs. Many school fairs have rules regarding table size and chair use. Similarly, most schools have rules about the use of electronic games, whether music is allowed, and having food or drink on the floor, as well as requirements for the students' nearness to their project, particularly during the judging process.

8: How Do I Put It All Together?

Other guides to doing a science fair project begin with this section instead of waiting until the end. However, I believe it is more important to know first what it takes to create a really good science fair project before thinking about putting together all of the components.

Additionally, some instructional guides describe the experimental process as if it is linear. It is not. Your idea for a project, the controls you have to consider, and the procedures you use can change and certainly should be revised as you move through the process.

What should go on a project backboard? These are the basic elements:

Project Title. Some students make their title cute. It's OK to do that, but using a "big" science word in your title is even better. For example, if you are doing a project with pumpkins it would be good to use the botanical name for the pumpkin (i.e., Cucurbitaceae) in the title.

Purpose and/or Problem Statement. This is more or less a short summary of what you did, and more importantly, why.

Hypothesis. Textbooks like to define *hypothesis* as an "educated guess." This is true, but it is good if you can explain in your hypothesis why you are making this "guess" as to the outcome. Your "guess" should be based on previous research or, at a minimum, a logical reason.

Variables. The independent/manipulated variable is the variable you manipulated to see if it made a change in the data.

Some examples:

Independent/Manipulated Variable	Project Description
String length	Changing the string length of a pendulum to see if this changes the rate.
Water	Changing water amounts to determine if this changes plant growth rate.
Popcorn brands	Changing brands of popcorn to see which one pops the most kernels.

The dependent/responding variable is the variable you measure, such as changes over time, a total number, length/height, etc.

Some examples:

Dependent/Responding Variable	Project Description
Swings/minute	Changing the string length of a pendulum to see if this changes the rate.
Plant growth	Changing water amounts to determine if this changes plant growth rate.
Number of kernels popped	Changing brands of popcorn to see which one pops the most kernels.

The controls are the variables you keep the same. I like to say that if you control for everything, you are a good scientist.

Some examples:

Controls	Project Description
Pendulum weight, drop angle, amount of time	Changing the string length of a pendulum to see if this changes the rate.
Amount of soil, location, type of plants, watering time, water temperature	Changing water amounts to determine if this changes plant growth rate.
Bag size, temperature, heating time	Changing brands of popcorn to see which one pops the most kernels.

Experimental Procedure. Write this as a step-by-step guide to your process. Include amounts, time, number of trials, and controls in the details. The more details the better.

Results/Data. The results/data should be in table format, and this section is also where you include your graphs. Some teachers require students to maintain a logbook of their data. This is something scientists do to track changes in growth, time, etc. Also, to keep your backboard from looking too crowded you may want to only display your graph(s).

Conclusion/Discussion/Recommendations. This section should be a summary of what occurred in your experiment. Was your hypothesis correct? Explain why or why not. Discuss what you could do to improve to your project. What are some expansions or additional questions/experiments you might consider beyond what you found out from this project?

Epilogue: Why Do a Science Fair Project?

Why do a science fair project? Perhaps I should have begun the book by answering that question. But I guess I considered that if you're reading this, you must realize that doing a science fair project has some kind of value for your child. If that is your belief, I agree with you on many levels.

As a university professor, I have for years given future elementary school teachers a specific assignment that tells me their thoughts on doing—and in some cases not doing—a science fair project as a child. The assignment, called a "science autobiography," asks them to write about science as related to their K-12 experiences. After reading these autobiographies for more than 25 years I have found that one of the more memorable elementary experiences for students was doing a science fair project. I have even had some students tell me that doing a science fair project is the only thing they remember about their elementary grades. Now, the science fair experience was not always pleasant for some, but it is something they definitely remember having to do. As a teacher I get a sense of satisfaction that students will remember something from my classes that stays with them for many years into the future.

What are other benefits of doing a science fair project? I think one is that it gets students to start thinking like scientists, and more importantly it shows them that they can do science. Another major benefit of science fair participation is that if your child sticks with it into high school, the awards given can increase considerably. As a previous state science fair director I witnessed high school students receive technology awards (e.g., computers), monetary awards (e.g., $1,000 savings bonds), and full college scholarships to prestigious universities across the United States.

Will reading this book result in your child winning ribbons, trophies, and other prizes? Unfortunately I can't make that promise. What I can promise is that if you follow the recommendations in this book, your child will learn what it means to think like a scientist, know what it takes to meet the requirements for a quality science fair project, and create a lasting lifelong memory.

Made in the USA
Columbia, SC
12 November 2022